Everyone has to go to hospital at some time in their life. We've all been. Would you like to know what our visits were for?

Note to parents
Learning to overcome the mixed feelings of a visit to a hospital can be very difficult for children. Their feelings (both good and bad) are often the result of previous visits and the influence they receive from others, including from media such as television. It is very important to introduce children to the reasons why we have hospitals, and rather than associate them with illness to show that they are part of the process of maintaining good health.

Children's experiences of hospitals vary from visits for their own treatment to accompanying adults when they visit friends and relatives. In this book we look at Emily and her family, and show just some of the things which happen during a visit to the hospital.

The author
Clare Devane-Caveney RGN OHNC is a nurse who works in Manchester.

Visit to the Hospital

written by Clare Devane-Caveney
illustrated by Lynne Byrnes

Copyright © 1991 World International Publishing Ltd.
All rights reserved. Published in Great Britain by
World International Publishing Ltd., an Egmont Company,
Egmont House, PO Box 111, Great Ducie Street,
Manchester M60 3BL. Printed in Germany.
ISBN 0 7498 0116 6

A CIP catalogue record for this book is available from the British Library

I had to visit the hospital when I fell off the swing in our garden. My arm hurt a lot and there was a cut on my knee.

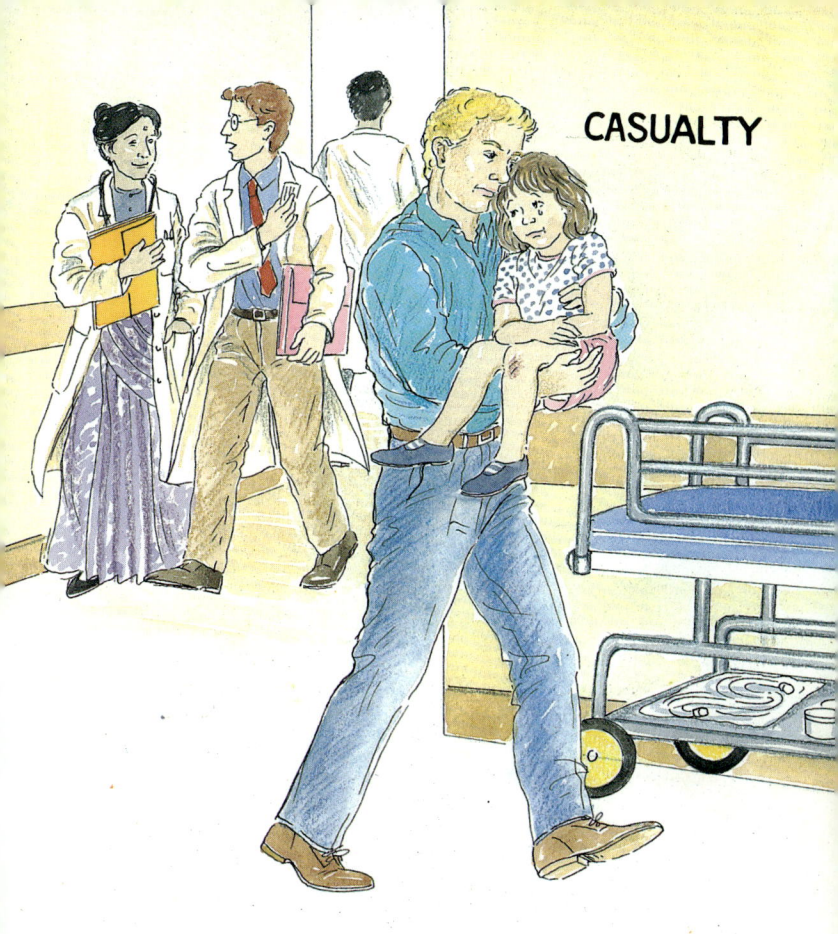

Daddy took me to the hospital. It had long corridors. The doctors and nurses were walking very quickly.

We went to the Casualty Department and waited in a room with other people. Then a doctor examined me. She had cold hands but she was very kind.

A nurse put a bandage on my knee. She said that this would stop it bleeding. The doctor said I had to have an X-ray to see if my arm was broken.

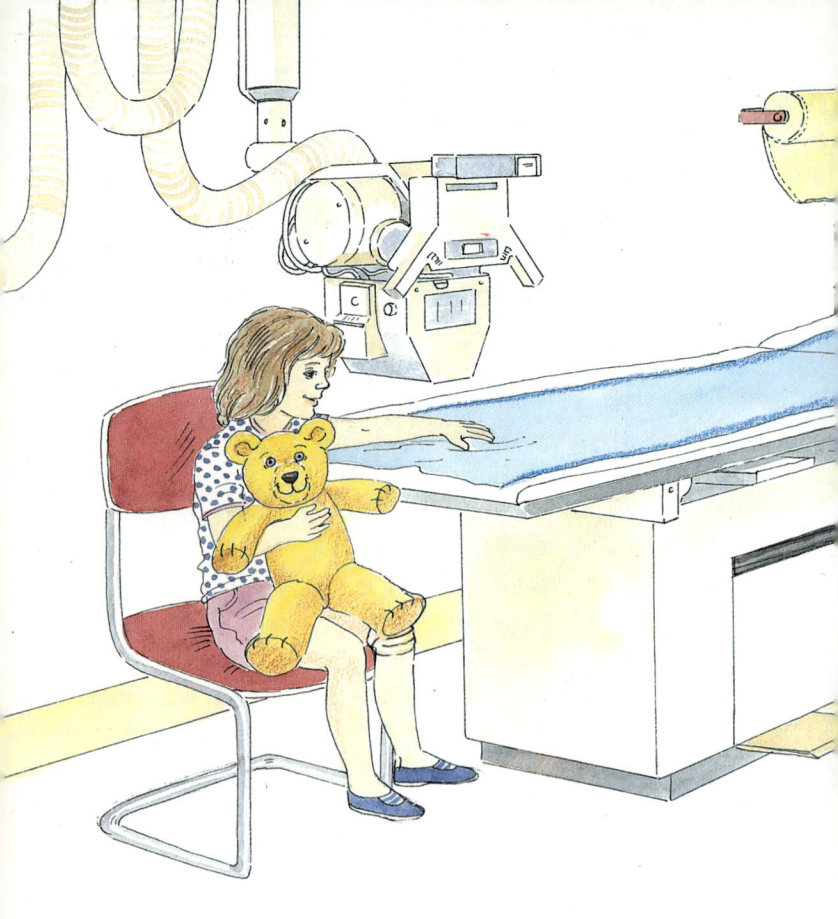

Daddy had to wait outside while the X-ray was taken. The nurse said that an X-ray was a photograph of a bone.

The nurse gave me a teddy to hold. The X-ray machine was placed over my arm to take the photograph. It didn't hurt.

The doctor said that my arm was broken.
A nurse took Daddy and me to the
Fracture Clinic.

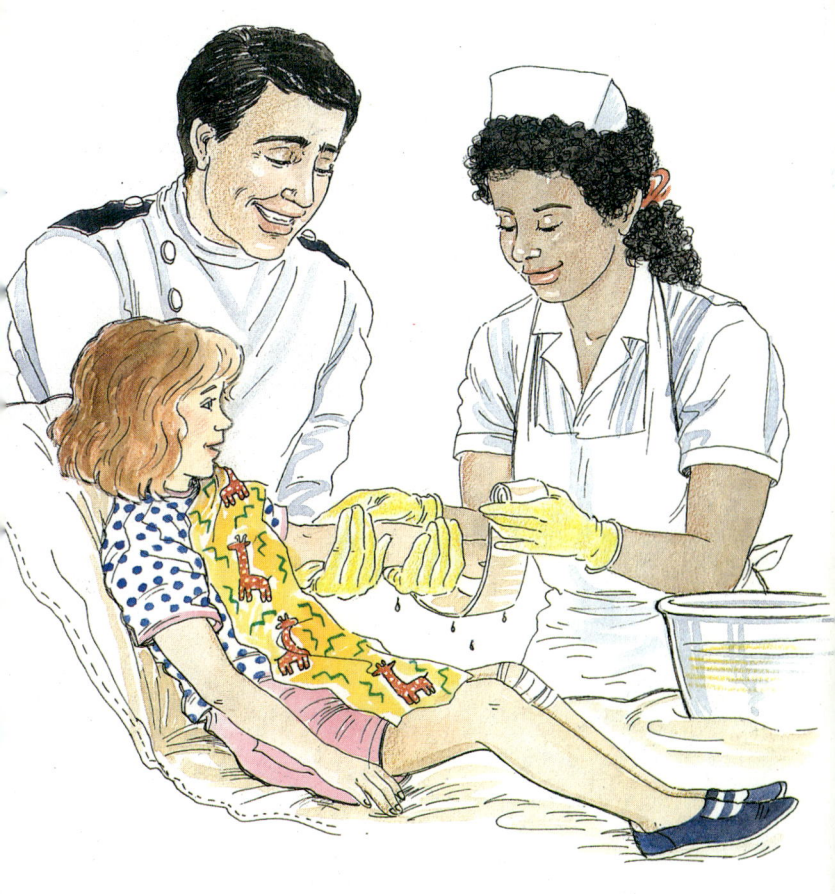

My arm was put in plaster. The plaster was all wet at first. Then it went very hard. The nurse said the plaster would help the bone fit back together again.

I had to have a tetanus injection, to stop germs from getting into the cut on my knee. I sat on Daddy's lap. I was scared even though it was a small needle.

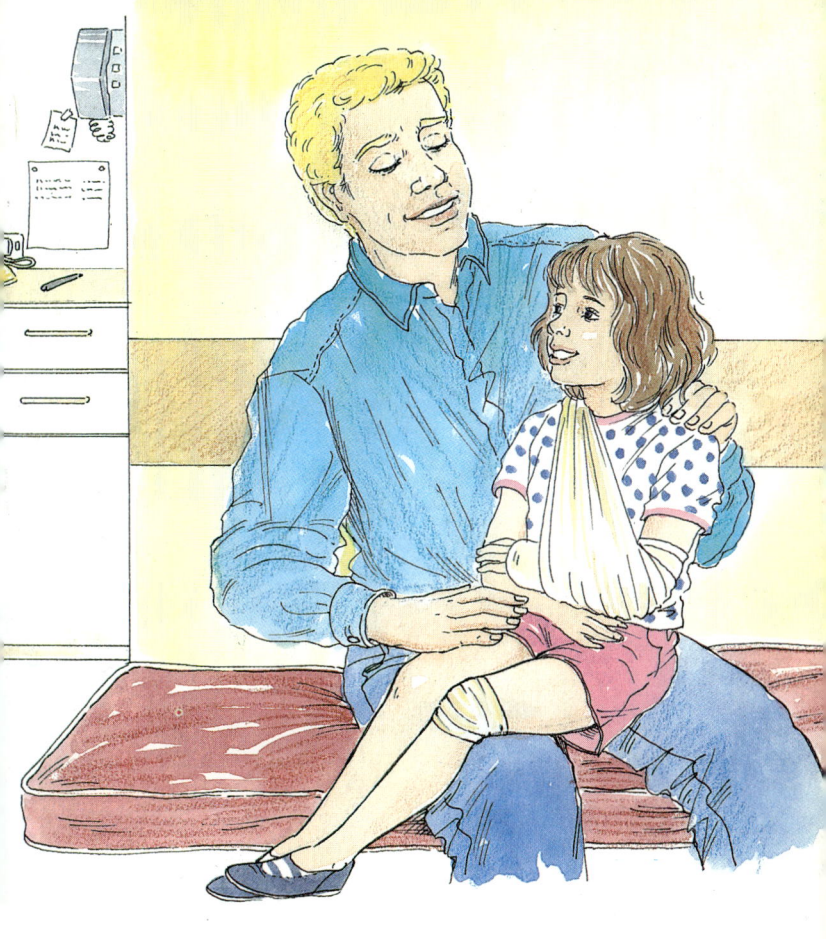

I cried a little bit. I don't like injections.
The nurse said that it would make my
knee better. He pulled a funny face and
made me laugh.

Last winter my Grandad was in hospital.
We went to visit him every week.

He was very ill. The doctors and nurses made him well again.

When he was better we all went to bring Grandad home. He had to go to the Pharmacy to collect his tablets.

You must never eat tablets or drink medicines at home, unless Mummy or Daddy give them to you. In our house they are in a high cupboard, out of reach.

My cousin Peter had an operation. The doctor gave him special air to breathe. It made him feel sleepy. His Mummy stayed until he was asleep. It didn't take long.

When he woke up his operation was over. He felt happy because his Mummy was by his bed. She read him a story. Then he played with the other children.

Auntie Lucy went to hospital to find out why she sneezed a lot when we went for walks in the country. She had an allergy test. Cousin Peter went with her.

The nurse pricked Auntie Lucy's arm and put different drops on it. She gave her special tablets to take. After a few weeks, Auntie Lucy didn't sneeze any more.

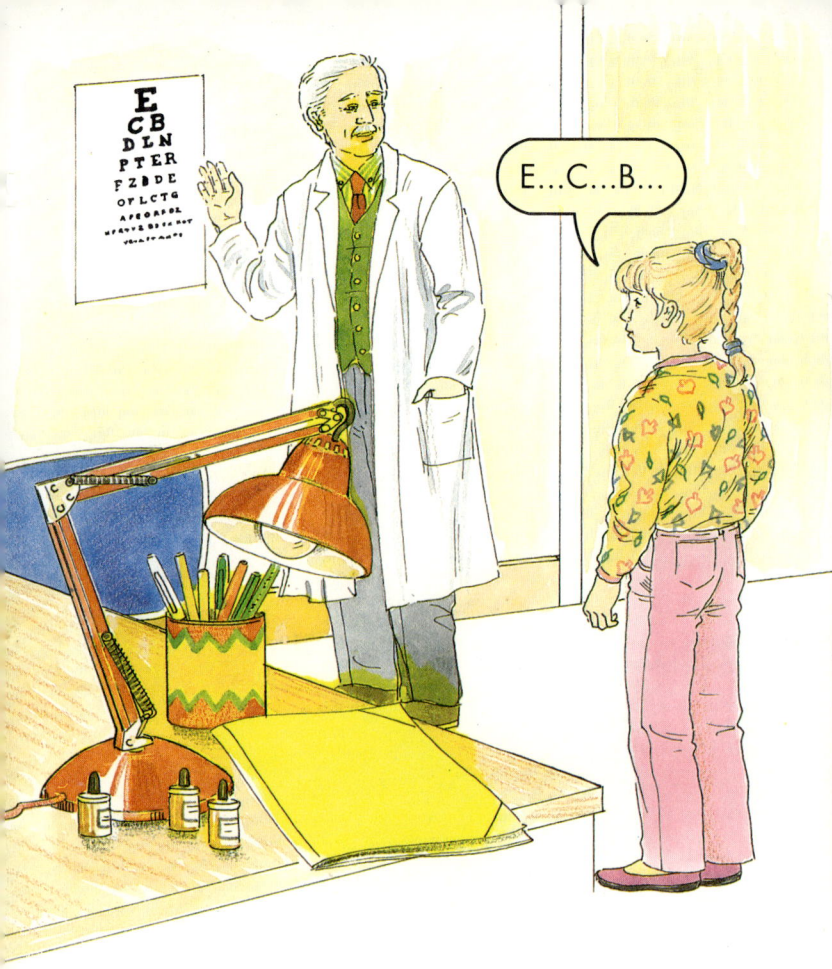

My sister Paula went to see a doctor who knew about eyes. She had to read letters from a card that was hanging on a wall.

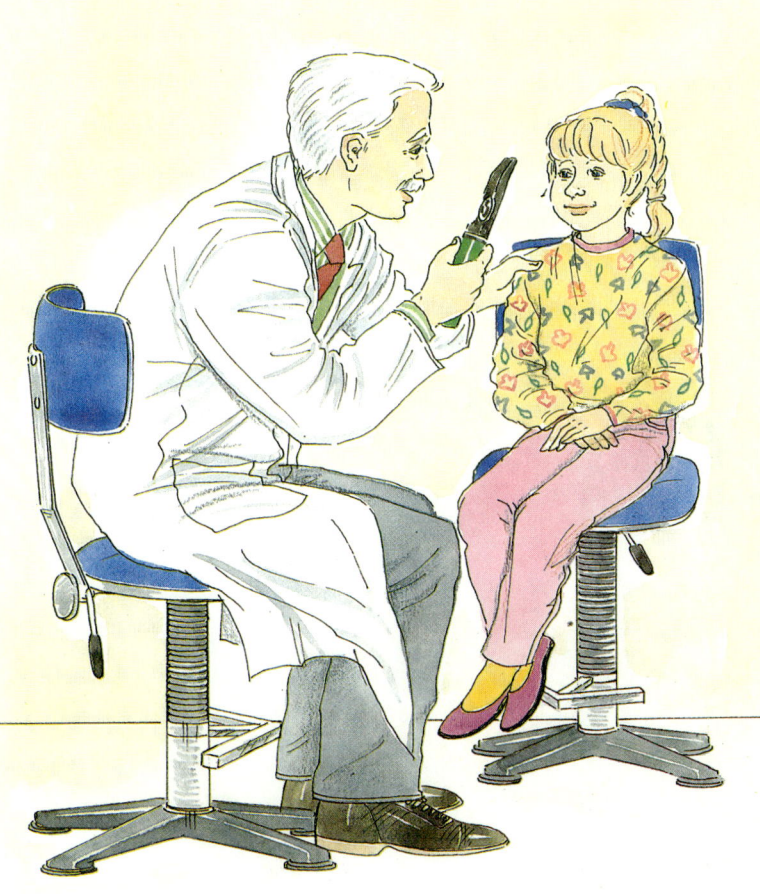

The doctor looked into her eyes with a bright light. Paula came home with new glasses. My Gran wears glasses.

Uncle Steven hurt his leg while playing football. He had to go to the hospital to learn special exercises. He had to stand on his tip-toes. Can you stand on yours?

He had to practice walking up and down stairs. Now he can play football again.

Hospitals are good places.
We've all been there and we feel better.